Dog Applause

Let's Hear It For

Boxers

Written by

Piper Welsh

Rourke
Educational Media

rourkeeducationalmedia.com

Scan for Related Titles
and Teacher Resources

www.rourkeeducationalmedia.com

PHOTO CREDITS: Cover: © Catherine Murray; page 4: © Daniela Jakob; page 5: © Fesus Robert; page 6: © James Boardman; page 7: © designpics (Great Dane), © Bonzami Emmanuelle (Rottweiler), © Eric Isselee (Siberian Husky); page 8: © Dkcphotography; page 9: © Dmitry Kalinovsky; page 10, 16: Lynn M. Stone; page 11: © Catherine Murray; page 13: © Brad Johnson; page 14: © Eric Isselee (Boston Terrier, English Bulldog), © Innaastakhova (Bull Mastiff); page 15: © Dmitry Kalinovsky; page 17: © Donna Kilday; page 18: © Coroiu Octavian; page 19: © Timothy OLeary; page 20: © Jose Gil; page 21: © Janabehr; page 22: © Eric Isselee

Edited by: Precious McKenzie

Cover design by: Renee Brady
Interior design by: Ashley Morgan

Library of Congress PCN Data

Welsh, Piper.
  Let's Hear It For Boxers / Piper Welsh.
    p. cm. -- (Dog Applause)
  Includes index.
  ISBN 978-1-62169-869-2 (hardcover)
  ISBN 978-1-62169-764-0 (softcover)
  ISBN 978-1-62169-970-5 (e-Book)
Library of Congress Control Number: 2013936480

Also Available as:

Rourke Educational Media
Printed in the United States of America,
North Mankato, Minnesota

Rourke
Educational Media

rourkeeducationalmedia.com

customerservice@rourkeeducationalmedia.com • PO Box 643328 Vero Beach, Florida 32964

Table of Contents

A handsome, athletic dog, Boxers make excellent family pets.

Boxers

Many people don't know it, but Boxers are among the most playful dogs. Boxer owners say that most Boxers are always puppies at heart, even as they get older.

But there is another side to a Boxer's personality. Boxers are fearless, and they are suspicious of strangers. Those characteristics, especially in male Boxers, make them useful guard dogs. Their muscular build and size also make them good guardians.

Boxer Facts

Weight:	50-80 pounds (23-36 kilograms)
Height:	21-25 inches (54-64 centimeters)
Country of Origin:	Germany
Life Span:	8-10 years

No one is quite sure where the Boxer got its name. It may be from the dog's habit of rearing up and jabbing at another Boxer with its forelegs.

Boxers must have plenty of outside playtime. They are among the most active and robust breeds.

Great Dane

Siberian Husky

Rottweiler

Many common breeds of dogs are members of the working dog group.

The Boxer is grouped with several other **breeds** of dogs in the working dog group. That is based largely on the work that Boxers did many, many years ago as hunting dogs and **bull-baiters**. A few Boxers are used today as working guard dogs. Most, though, are kept as family companions.

Look at Me!

The Boxer has a short, square, black **muzzle**. It has long legs, a deep chest, and a stubby tail. It has a wrinkled forehead.

First look at a Boxer and you will find the dog to be sophisticated, aloof, and reserved.

Square-jawed and muscular, the Boxer is a beautiful dog who requires a lot of exercise.

Ideally, Boxers are either fawn colored with some white or **brindled** and white. Brindled Boxers are tan or brown with some striping.

All-white Boxers are fairly common, but they cannot be show dogs. They often have more health problems than other Boxers.

North American Boxers usually have sharp, upright ears. Upright ears are not natural. Boxer pups are born with floppy ears. To get upright ears, Boxer pups undergo minor ear surgery called **cropping**. Then their ears are taped upright for at least one month.

Many Boxers have docked tails and cropped ears.

All white or mostly white Boxers are not desired because genetically, deafness is associated with white coloring.

In England, cropping of Boxer ears is against the law. Boxers keep their floppy ears. Some American owners would prefer that their Boxers keep their floppy ears, too.

History of the Boxer

In the 1700s, German dog breeds known as Bullenbaisers were used by hunters to chase and grab large game animals with their strong jaws. These dogs were strong but quick.

Bullenbaisers had short **muzzles**, or noses, that helped

them to breathe easily while they clung with their teeth to the deer or wild boar. The dogs were also used to attack bulls in a former sporting event.

Boxers started becoming popular in the U.S. in the late 1940s when soldiers coming home from World War II brought their Boxer mascots with them.

Around 1830, German hunters began to develop a new breed. They used Bullenbaisers along with terriers, large mastiffs, and finally bulldogs.

Boston Terrier

English Bulldog

Bullmastiff

By breeding different breeds of dogs with complimentary characteristics dog breeders created new breeds, such as Boxers.

A Boxer's short nose and short hair make them uncomfortable in hot and cold weather, which is why they are better as house dogs.

Boxers and Bulldogs have two things in common. They both drool and snore a lot!

The end result, by 1895, was the Boxer. In 1904, the Boxer was accepted by the American Kennel Club (AKC) as a new breed. Since then, the Boxer has grown in populartity across the United States. The AKC announced, in early 2013, that the Boxer was the seventh most popular breed in the United States.

A Boxer's conformation and regal appearance make it popular within the dog show circuit.

A Loyal Companion

The Boxer is a popular dog for good reasons. It's handsome, athletic, and full of personality. It also has a short, shiny fur coat that does not require constant brushing.

Boxers require very little grooming but even with their short fur, they still shed quite a bit.

Boxers are renowned for their great love of and loyalty to their families.

Boxers are not easy dogs to care for. They are active dogs, and they require active owners. Because a Boxer can be stubborn, it needs an owner with a kind, but firm, hand.

Boxers are generally good with children, but some Boxers are **aggressive** toward other dogs.

Proper daily excercise will keep a Boxer happy and keep its owner happy, too!

A Boxer needs daily exercise, either in a large, fenced yard or on a long walk or jog with its owner. And because they do not do well in either hot or cold weather, Boxers need time indoors. Once indoors, however, their size and puppy personality can be very difficult for their owners to accept.

Boxers are playful dogs that can make great companions if you have patience and can take the time to train them.

When a Boxer gets regular exercise, it is able to relax and get into less mischief when it is indoors.

Doggie Advice

Puppies are cute and cuddly, but only after serious thought should anybody buy one. Puppies grow up.

Choosing the right breed requires some homework. And remember that a dog will require more than love and patience. It will need healthy food, exercise, grooming, a warm, safe place in which to live, and medical care.

A dog can be your best friend, but you need to be its best friend, too.

For more information about buying and owning a dog, contact the American Kennel Club at *www.akc.org/index.cfm* or the Canadian Kennel Club at *www.ckc.ca/*.

Glossary

aggressive (uh-GRES-siv): wanting to attack or attacking

breeds (BREEDZ): particular kinds of domestic animals within a larger, closely related group, such as the Boxer breed within the dog group

brindled (BRIN-duld): having hard-to-see streaks of dark color on a lighter background

bull-baiters (BUHL BAYT-urz): dogs that were used to attack and bite bulls in a ring or arena

cropping (CROP-ping): the minor surgery that removes part of an animal's ear

muzzle (MUZ-zul): the nose and jaws of animals; a snout

Index

Websites to Visit

www.akc.org/breeds/boxer

www.dogbreedinfo.com/boxer.htm

www.dogster.com/dog-breeds/Boxer

Show What You Know

1. In what year did the American Kennel Club recognize the Boxer as a breed?
2. Why does a Boxer need an owner with a firm hand?
3. What grouping of dog is the Boxer in?